VERSUS

Versus

WILLIAM VALLIÈRES

THE POETRY IMPRINT AT VÉHICULE PRESS

Published with the generous assistance of The Canada Council for the Arts and the Canada Book Fund of the Department of Canadian Heritage, and the Société de développement des entreprises culturelles du Québec (SODEC).

Canada Council   Conseil des arts
for the Arts   du Canada

Canadä

SODEC
Québec

SIGNAL EDITIONS EDITOR: CARMINE STARNINO

Cover design: David Drummond
Photo of the author by Michael Shu
Set in Filosofia and Minion by Simon Garamond
Printed by Marquis Book Printing Inc.

Dépôt légal, Library and Archives Canada and the Bibliothèque national du Québec, third trimester 2019.

LIBRARY AND ARCHIVES CANADA CATALOGUING IN PUBLICATION

Title: Versus / William Vallières.

Names: Vallières, William, author.

Description: Poems.

Identifiers: Canadiana (print) 20190157534 | Canadiana (ebook) 20190157542 | ISBN 9781550655322

(softcover) | ISBN 9781550655377 (EPUB)

Classification: LCC PS8643.A4495 V47 2019 | DDC C811/.6—dc23

Published by Véhicule Press, Montréal, Québec, Canada
www.vehiculepress.com

Distributed in Canada by LitDistCo
www.litdistco.ca

Distributed in the U.S. by Independent Publishers Group
www.ipgbook.com

Printed in Canada

For Seb

CONTENTS

versus (prep.):
from Latin *versus* "turned toward or against," from
past participle of *vertere* "to turn, turn back, be turned,
convert, transform, translate, be changed."

Sowings

I sank in the field
That bordered our backyard
It had rained and was raining still
When I borrowed the muddy ground

I plodded through the drills
All perpendicular to my journey
Till a puddle pulled
A red boot off

Perched on one foot, sock half
Dangling off the other
I looked to home, not far off
And pushed a few high hatchling-shouts

A light came on in the kitchen
Behind me, dusk was being born
Seed spuds, like bone white stones
Marked my passing

Picture

The family in late August greenness
Shadows on the lawn trawling duskward
Grandfather there, François too, sipping Blue
Little cousins biting cobs in the nude
Grandmother graced with glowing daughters
Uncles filling the pool with rivalry and nerve
Beyond the fence, stalks cutting strong and upward

Pennies

Back after university
I bumped into him by the fountain
The old cracked thing that spat
Mostly mist by then, where he spent
Most days waiting
Shaking
Among pigeons and the very old
Under the market awning

He asked for a ten
I gave it
He asked for a smoke and I gave that too
Two cousins again
We watched the vacant workday afternoon

He took a good long drag
"We used to toss pennies in there, remember"

I remember the cold, clear water
Dunking our hands for the loot
Picking the ones that winked like lures
And casting them back again, charged

But told him I didn't
Unwilling to succumb
To how they gleamed in there
The brackish pool
Where everything seemed to accumulate

Smokes and rain, feathers, fates

Gare Centrale

The noise here rises like a hymn
To the vaulted ceiling
It rises and is suffused
With the light dragged through
The high windows

People gather under numbers
Check their phones
And disperse
Lugging belongings
Like penitents to an empty church

A woman sits by an open umbrella
Blowing on coffee, ankles crossed
The shoe shiner watches from the darkness of his door
A faceless, floating
Apron-square of white

He learned to tell time
From the faces of strangers
Tell me, my friend
How many faces make up the hour?
Many, my friend, many

Meanwhile somewhere
A train travels fast
Along the ditch-grass
Bound forever
To Gare Centrale

Kill Poem

I found a mouse
Caught in the trap
I killed the mouse
With quick little taps

Its shrieks were squeaks
To my human ears
Tap tap tap
With my boot heel

The mouse man came
With all his poisons
Little pink pellets
Is what was chosen

Now no mice
Move through the walls
Now no mice
Bother to call

Little pink pellets
Little pink pills
It's all very human
I don't have to kill

No mice in the walls
Means I can work
Tap tap, a poem
Tap tap, this verse

Spring

The sun bursts like a gong
Struck by a god
Dragging everyone, everywhere
To consciousness again

Birds slap together nests
Of sprig and plastic
Squirrels raid
Long-looted caches

I know those blank, panicked eyes
When I lift the barbecue lid and find one nesting
When daylight bears down on you
At once, like a verdict

Dazed, innocent
Pried from winter's rooms
We go bumping into each other
Politely

New Year's Eve

I outlive David Bowie
And Zsa Zsa Gabor
I outlive Prince
Fidel Castro
Carrie Fisher and Debbie Reynolds

I suck back oysters
Hoisted to my lips
By men I do not know
The raw clots fizzle
In my stomach full of foam

Five, four, three, two, one…
I drain my glass to the stem
I'm draining light from a gem
I drink and see my death
Get smaller and smaller

It shrinks to the size of an embryo
It shrinks to almost zero
It shrinks and is dissolved
Into my ego—tonight, I swallow
The black yolk whole

Today I Join François

Grandfather would rock
In the corner of the kitchen
Didn't speak much, just rocked
Back and forth in thought

Once, when Grandmother was making coffee
He shot up to shout
"I've had enough! I'm going to kill myself!
Today I join François!"

She rolled her eyes, stopped counting
And asked, "What do you expect from it?
What will you do? Sit with him in heaven
And drink coffee all day and chat?"

He proclaimed, eyes wide
"Not coffee—champagne!"
And shuffled, in his long johns, down the hall, off to bed
"He's just tired" she said

But we knew how it was—
When the coffee was ready
We raised our cups
To the next best thing

At Baptism

A bat flapped
In the church corner dark
A wing mangled bad

We watched it flop round its wound
Attempting flight
But striking ground between the pews

Blind to us, deaf to the noise our tongues made
Its seeking pitch
Mapped us

Above
The human form
Descending

This Poem is Not Short

I don't trust short men
They want what I got
In the metro they huddle
Like weasels under my arm

Hitler, Stalin, Napoleon
These were all short men
Would you let their little hands
Grab the helm?

My dentist is short
My boss is too
Tom Cruise is short
He wears elevator shoes

This is why short men schmooze
One has to drink a lot of booze
To be fucked by a man
In elevator shoes

I drink a lot of booze
I would fuck Tom Cruise
In his elevator shoes, on tiptoes
He might just reach my A-hole

He'd squeal a squirrel's
Shrill mating call
Having him in me, like flinging
A weenie down a hall

Seconds later, once he was done
I'd lie and say I had fun
Why not? After all
Give them an inch and they'll still be small

The world is full of little short men
Who need our little white lies
The world is full of little white lies
Because of their little white size

Size doesn't matter
That's the biggest lie of all
Just look at this poem
It's ten stanzas tall

Third Rehab

I drove him home

He smoked like a veteran
Cracking jokes
About the saps still stuck in there
Their slowness
The spark that won't catch
When asked a simple question

"And Tommy, the cowboy who can only stomach coke?
He smashed his car into the home
There's no hope for that guy, no hope," he said
Laughing through his smoke
As the dark streets led
From houses with little porch lights on
To his building full of rooms
Locked along dim halls
And the dreaded walk to his own

Poupées Russes

Monday, we are trapped in our own breasts
Tuesday, we are but a little bit less
Wednesday, the toughest's shed
We are halfway to the rest
Thursday, we're pregnant
With Friday, the best
Because the week-
End's next, when
We get to flex
What's left:
A nug-
get

In Sleep

In my black noon
Whims dress and undress
And dance like fools
They never sweat the daylight rules

But when dawn rouses light from the brink
Once again, I spend
My being being
Everything I'm against

The Only Land is Disneyland

Strew black garlands at the door
And paint the last sign white
There's medicine but no cure
The only land is Disneyland

The long shadow has been solved
In beige and shades of mauve
Kiss the acclimated, kiss them goodnight
The only land is Disneyland

Bear the rat's song
Bidden at the break of day
Burn Februar into your heart
The only land is Disneyland

Lift the styrofoam cup
Break it as bread
Let the dead thing crest
The only land is Disneyland

When I Was a Boy

Manicured and permed
The youngest Aunts yearned
Over catalogues all day
Every page, every page, every page
Watching the three of us
My cousins and me
While our mothers had to work

And while our mothers had to work
We were the boys out back
Enacting movies we were weaned on
The point was to free the good guy's girl
Bound in the bad guy's bunker

My cousins bickered for the bad guy role
Bold and dark, handsome and wrong
Getting it done with brawn

I preferred to be the blonde
Helpless, gagged
But half the job

Painted with a desperate cry
I'd crawl through the dog house hole
And await a foe or hero's face

I'd kick and squirm, plead and bawl
Live and die
Till lunch was called

We played our parts
Till mom came back from the packing plant
Smelling like blood, like the inside of a can

Nights, we watched the blondes on TV
Until it was bedtime for me
The little man of the house
Carried delicately off-screen

Ill Will

I bristle in my seat
As the kiddies on scene
Repeat their prosy
Look-at-me kind of poetry

I send in the pit of me
Bones to pick clean
The pile seeps
Putrid to the spleen

... Once I started sporting seventeen leeks
My instagram blew up.
The only horror in this world is being a surfing werewolf.
I serenade burritos with a lute...

I chew my cheek
In the bar's dark reaches
Dropping sick spondees
Only my mother will read

The Light

for B. Kennedy

I suck the soup straight out of the can
The mailbox is full of small, pressing debts
When I go to parties
People have very important and modern problems
Good riddance to conclusions
But mostly how they come about
Let me tell you about starting over
Like the window you seek morning from
Everybody looks through you
Letting in the light

How Oysters Do It

Stuck
In their bone-husks
At the bottom of the sea
Off the green, lighted coast
Where picnickers greet the wide wind with toasts
They sift with their glot
Picking sustenance from salt
The good from the bad
Choking the crap
To hard, neutering pearl

Rue Panet

Shut inside our fuchsia kitchen
Drinking to the evening's radio
A chicken roasting in the oven
We catted about our loves and lays
Bartenders, postmen, aspiring veterinarians
And that mister dismissed
With a flick of your quick, decisive wrist
How things get rowdy when a man loves another!
The neighbours were from France and fighting
About marriage or margarine, we never knew
And you would roll your big brown eyes
"Have you really seen people love each other in this city?"
By the window, pining to Carole King
We drank our mouths to a Beaujolais bruise
Wondering who would have us
The way we had ourselves
Those first few years on Panet

Nightfeed

The park at night is no one
The trail is cast with shadows bent
On the asking shape of others

Downhill, as if rolled out of a nest
The stadium glows
Like an egg with the moon inside it

I mark your approach
Soon, in your heat, there is nothing
Besides you in the dark

A warm yellow centre
Mornings, when I scoop it out
It trickles like you did

I Became a Fabulous Opera

I sang to a sea of mouths
In stadiums named after banks and cola

I wore gowns made of Burger King receipts
Badger meat bikinis
Blazers with increasingly large epaulettes

I soaked in Himalayan yak milk
After the show
To cleanse me of their gazes

I was everything, I was everywhere

The label often sent
American men who pleased me
I ate fish with bare hands on a beach with Brent
Connected the dots on a freckled Pete
Sported dildos that made Brandons weep

I stopped dedicating autographs
Because the names were too ugly
I had cantaloupes flown fresh from Capri
I bought a ranch
And bred prize-winning steeds there

I'm telling you this because life is short

Copula

The night is a velvet knot
That will resolve itself in thunder
Every window is a gaping mouth
Wide, wanting, waiting

Listen—*ugh, ugh*—
The real thing or porn?
The city makes it hard
To avoid what others want

On the other side of this court
A match is rubbed to moisture
And further, past the cries of cats
The pow of boxcars coupling

The banana on the counter bulges brown
The ceiling fan whisks heat to a tizzy
What was it I wanted
Before I wanted this?

Dear Milosz

The day's adopted blue
And the river and the oak tree hold splendour
But it is hard
When one is very busy
And must get home from the office as quickly as one can
But idles instead in red streams of light
In winter's bleakening pre-dusk
To share your sense of reverent wonder
So tell me
Did you really rest your head against a cold clear pane
And behold dawn hit the hills magenta?
Did the thrush really sing at your sill?
Or was it all invoked
Like the oak tree was
Long ago, by the river?

Luminescence

It's rare that I'm up before you
Rare to hear kids kick the crusted ice
Neighbours slamming doors and handling keys

I check the internet
Shrinking caps, what a star said on twitter, the earth flat again
I shut the laptop and open a book

When you wake with little eyes, I make toast
Put the jam on the table
And we talk about the movie we watched last night

How it was beautiful, furtive and real
Not unlike a dream
As I wash strawberries in December

Above a Broken Toilet

At the first flush, it will not flush
And the landlord, in Miami
Sipping cocktails with the rent he wrung from us
Can't get to it for weeks

Each morning, I ponder last night's supper
Brown going down
But then back up
Wondering, when did I have peanuts?

Or thoughts like these: galaxies swirl in a similar fashion
In the meaningless void of space
And absolutely everything, on the level of the atom
Is infinite and equal—it takes

Nothing but chance alignments
To make Doris Day not a turd
A landlord not a poet
Peanuts never birds

But ultimately, it's our ability
To perceive this that's important
There are many ways to be
But ours comes with discernments

Rock and Roll

I cut my feet
Twisting and shouting
Goddamn obscenities on the hardwood floor

Just a riff of thee
And my teeth numb
My throat accepts thrilling smoke
Beer shuts up my bones
I crave in chorus

I have neglected family, friends
And the classics of literature and philosophy
For your teenage Marx
And middle-aged Jesus

I went to church
And bought what I was sold

I forgive you
You were always there for me
Even tonight
When my boyfriend's not into you
And all my friends are texts

Who needs loneliness

Fuck it
Fuck it till it all bends to grace

When Rodrigo Comes Home

Here we are shirtless, Rodrigo and I
Gruff among the pies and stews
Two portly kings in the kitchen riding
The polka station's giddy groove

Rodrigo's no hombre home by five
Rodrigo trucks the long haul routes
Through snows of both Dakotas, California fires
With a burdened box just for you

But all that ends with me tonight
And our bellies brushing in the moonlight blue
So ladle some daddy, grab another slice
Tomorrow, together, we sleep off the asphalt, the diesel, the lube

Instructions for Tomato Sandwich

Toast the bread till tan lines show
Nothing more than a starting crunch
Enough to keep the inner fluff
Safe from the gush to come

Pinch the tomato's green bud crown
Tilt it on its own ripe bulge
Slice the summer thing slowly
Eat the butt-cheek bit

Mortar the toast with mayo
Fan four slices out
Add salt and pepper
Then seal the meal

Note, O sandwich maker, the most important part
A tomato is a monthful of rain
If once assembled, you don't eat it up
Summer soaks through the grain

Poem for My Grandmother

When I heard you were sick
You became the little girl you told me of
The one who used to hide in the hay
In the red and white barn
When it was time for her
To do the dishes after supper
And I became the little boy you told that story to
And I hid with you in the hay
Listening to your father's voice
Booming through the rafters
As the summer days were fading
And the dishes were piling up

Drifting Snow

How are you?
Thank you for the roses
They'll be nice in vases

The last time we spoke
Something was new
What's different?

Between me and the drifting snow
There's nothing but a door

It is a door I must never exit

How easy it is
To stray from yourself

A city full of people
Stepping indifferently
Over a corpse

After

There comes a day of incredible clarity
The way the sun strikes exploded alps on the pane
And beyond, treetops, clicking crystal chandeliers

And you have nothing to say

Just a series of impressions pressed onto consciousness
A sudden aria of the head, the glance of a glance
Itself errant and the aim

Through Country

Autumn offers
Flushing shades of leaf
Plums, crimsons, amber-oranges
Tuck the tattered corn

Then long road
Through exploded boulder
Scrubbed aback
By what the winds wage

Dim cows on steep slopes
Puff and prod the greenery
Geese against the grey sky go
Altogether southward

On the shoulder, raccoons recur
Cuddling their innards
Radio thins like mist
And drowns

Static suggests
Nothing, nada
But there's ground to cover
Somewhere to be

Hearth

Outside, caught in a long wind's haul
Treetops shift in the off-milk dusk

Here, in a cottage booked in autumn woods
You sit by fire
A year into marriage

Log after log is put
To throw the night
Off into the corners

And through this light you see
Caked in years of soot
A man in low-relief
In the pit's back wall

Kneeling, he's presenting
A bushel to his wife

It's worth
The promise to transform it
Is the bread they'll break
By the hot tall hearth

You chuck another log on

The edge of light
Grows a bit
But beyond that, who knows

You uncork the good wine

Turin Horse

As steadily as it had clopped
The cobbled streets of Turin
Carting clerks to their desks, councilmen to their clubs
It stopped
In the heart of the piazza
One bitter January's start

Its master bid it go
But it would not budge

Wrapping the reins taut
He tugged them twice
But it would not budge

Unfurling his whip
He cracked it
A breath above its skull
But it would not budge

The driver knew the day would come
The horse was nearing thirteen
But not now, behind as he was
With the landlord, the grocer, the coalman, the bookies
And the kids in last year's trousers
And bread and broth nightly

Rising from the coach, he showed the beast no mercy
He lashed the horse's hips

Its back, its sides
Lashed it on the muzzle
Lashed it across the eyes

Still it would not budge

The horse only shuffled
Shook its clotted mane
And huffed into the cold morning
The last of what it had to give

The Kingfish

Leave where they are king
And swim inland
For a freshwater clearing

There, undermoon
The grim-lipped pilgrims
Spend hunted energy
And heartbeats that are counted
To swim in a senseless loop

No life-giving
No life-taking happens here

The Kingfish move
Scale to scale
Head to tail
Bobbing in the muscle-momentum
Circling nothing
To no end
But the means

The Cobblestones of Paris

1848

They were pulled one by one
And heaped into jagged spines
Laced with fissured pots, fractured spokes
And cut, rusty grating
Whatever the fighters could wrangle
Against the armed advance

The barricades slowed the soldiers down
But it was not enough
Rows of bayonets
Teeth in a great shark's mouth
Closed on the insurgents

1968

Sous les pavés, la plage!
The students chanted through their scarves
Beneath the cobblestones, the beach!
A new world
Where no king, no president, no businessman says
Obey, this is mine, shut up, pay!

They marched through parting gas
To rubber bullets and batons
Sous les pavés, la plage!
They shouted

Because de Gaulle looked tired
And the moment was right .

TODAY

The cobblestones are in their place
Where they haven't been paved over

Only plastic wrappers
Dance on them

Donkey Bridge

Go, damn donkey
Stop that rusty bray!
It's no sudden cliff
But trick of perspective, you see?
Beyond this hump
The bridge unfolds to the other shore gently
The water is wide
And thick with current
It's either back
Down the scorched path
Through the burning hills to ruin
Or getting over this
For greener pastures
There's only seeing the road for no road
That's holding us here

Who Will Take it From You

A prince feeds his falcons
Papaya on a private jet
As the attendant regrets
Her Liberal Arts education

A thousand overcoated clerks
Marching to Excel
Burp gluten-free toasts
Discreetly into their lapels

Pale young mavericks
In bachelor pads type
SHE DESERVED IT
The long, loveless night

Spackled are the stately domes!
Columnated ruins domino
As armoured Cadillacs roam
Washington when the sun goes down

Tell me, Mother, what is to be done
With The Man and his hacks
Who do not have our backs
And this time round, no rock & roll to save us?

Orwell at Barnhill

A stone, wind-worn swathe
Of low grass, crag-clutching shrub
And rough cliff
Cutting clean
To sea and sky
Locked in a lead horizon

He types in a lumpy bed
In near-dark hard for the eyes
The peat fire scarcely
Repelling the cold coming through

Rest will come
Between the speckling cough
And maiming medicine, it will come
But for now
It's bone, stone, and firmament

Milk And Honey

Nothing's alright in principle
But I'll be damned if I don't have it in me today
To grab everyone's hat
And twirl, screaming
J'ai ton chapeau! in a singsong way

Snow falls fat and mute around the lighted tower
Christmas will be soon
You're cubing mangoes by a candle in the nude

When will these four walls fall all around us
And roofs lift clean like pot lids
And we get plucked by the roiling storm
And never put down again?

The apprehensive bride and apprehensive groom
Smile in the shiny

The limousine's late or might not show at all

Late Hoorah

Winter has been long
Birches, stripped of bark
Shook along the lakeshore
Powder flew off roofs
Even the pug in boots
Once daintily promenading
No longer finds it cute

But Spring, after straying, returns
To the rousable, the sun speaks
Friends regain balconies
Neighbours, stoops
Hellos are uttered through naked hedge
There's sanity in what we feel
A commonness, a clearing

Aunt Francine

She went away
Into the basement
And never came back

What heavy voices
Ushered her in?
Was it like entering
A baptism of void?

She was the only grownup
To have ever given me a book
Peter Pan
And she signed it

She wore her long black hippy hair
In a braid down her back
There's a photo of her with flowers, crosslegged on the grass
Smiling with the secret demeanour
Of a librarian

She went from school to school
To teach children to brush their teeth
After she died
Coworkers were surprised to hear she smoked
Although she smoked all her life

There was no note
She was buried with a silk scarf

It was lovely to have known her

Funerals

The first one I was six
Chin propped on the back of the pew
Staring at the copper choir
Under windows
Gilding daylight through

Everyone faced a man with dentures
And Jesus on the cross—
What's this, I thought
The singing light anointing
Backs instead of brows?

~

I was twenty for the next one
Not wiser, but livid with his death
I sat in the same church
But this time saw the pillars for what they were:
Wood as hollow as bamboo
Painted to look like quartz
The mic'ed priest cooed
"I am the resurrection, and I am the life"
Under altar lights
Dimmed by settled dust
Later, as the low bell tolled
We gathered behind the gravedigger's crack
As he lowered the urn
With slackenings of the straps

Down beyond the spaded grass
Out of sight
Until a strap hissed loose
And François' ashes

Thudded
To the dug earth

∾

The last one (for now)
Was at a Funeral Complex

Grandmother's portrait
Captured as if humming
An old familiar song
Was bordered by still, unscented lilies

The place was made of glass
A bright, transparent box
I watched a cup get swept across
The sidewalk across the street

Young trees, new to the ground
And new to breezes
Submitted to them
As vast, mountainous clouds
Smuggled their emptiness past

When the service ended
We were led from the place of mourning

To a place where white, crustless sandwiches
Were laid on a table

Coffees in hand, coffee to warm us
We spoke of how it was
Paper platefuls of daily bread

Friday

What yesterday had fought to bud
Is stunted under ice today
Puddles are fixed
Mid-chop
Trees are shedding sleet
Birds in black, contorted branches
Shiver in their moulting
Tired and unrejoicing
Grey to grey more gradually
The day's like ash in water

But this is no day for dying
On channel 3, Moses splits
A technicolor sea
As Jesus on channel 10
Breaks bread with blue-eyed men
Months on bright display
Hollow chocolate eggs
Quiver for the day
Little teeth will crack
Their sweet, special shells
Some call this day good
And go about their buying
And wanting, and sighing
But this is no day for dying

ACKNOWLEDGEMENTS

Poems from this collection have appeared in *The Best Canadian Poetry in English 2019*, *The Walrus*, *Event*, *Grain*, and *The City Series: Montreal*. Thank you to the editors.

Thank you Niki Lambros, beacon of books, master of fire, friend. Thank you for coaxing the poet out of me.

Thank you Sarah Burgoyne. The drum is at your gate.

Thank you Jeff Noh, Paige Cooper, Kasia van Schaik, Jessi MacEachern, Tyler Morency, Casey Burkholder, Hilary Bergen, and Yann Geoffroy.

Thank you Stephanie Bolster, Mary di Michele, and Nicola Nixon, who endured a coarser version of this book.

Thank you Seb for putting up with me.

Thank you to my mother, my father, and my sister.

Merci, Lise, pour la sérénité de ton divan.

Thank you Carmine Starnino and everyone at Véhicule Press.